The Banquet of Donny & Ari

The Banquet of Donny & Ari

Scenes from the Opera

NAOMI GUTTMAN

Brick Books

Library and Archives Canada Cataloguing in Publication

Guttman, Naomi, 1960–, author
     The banquet of Donny & Ari : scenes from the opera / Naomi Guttman.

Issued in print and electronic formats.
ISBN 978-1-77131-351-3 (pbk.).—ISBN 978-1-77131-353-7 (pdf).—
ISBN 978-1-77131-352-0 (epub)

     I. Title II. Title: Banquet of Donny and Ari.

PS8563.U67B36 2015   C811'.54   C2014-907910-9
                                              C2014-907911-7

We acknowledge the Canada Council for the Arts, the Government of Canada through the Canada Book Fund, and the Ontario Arts Council for their support of our publishing program.

The author photo was taken by Sophie Kandaouroff.
The book is set in DTL Albertina.
Cover image by Shutterstock.
Design and layout by Marijke Friesen.

Printed and bound by Sunville Printco Inc.

Brick Books
431 Boler Road, Box 20081
London, Ontario N6K 4G6

www.brickbooks.ca

In Memory
Sharon Cynthia Herman Mead
and
Ron Gottesman

Contents

Prologue
    Hochelaga   5
    Early music   6
    Chernobyl wedding, 1986   7

Act I: Winter
    Argonautica   11
    Feast and famine   12
    Orchard and forest   13
    The clay we are made of   14
    Black leather couch   15
    The book of life   16
    Human Footprint Series: Artist's Statement   17
    Mouths of babes   18
    Domestic dirge   19
    Supermarket blues   20
    Water cycle   21
    Superhero lullaby   23
    By with it   24
    Backhoe   25
    Hospital solitaire   26
    Shiva   27
    In memoriam: Sonata 1014   28
    Fugue   29

Act II: Spring
    Thin wishes   33
    Minatory spring   34

Sour teeth 35
Lecture on the origins of music 36
The male gaze 37
Montreal limestone 38
None the wiser 39
For every lock a key 40
Perennial 41
Theories of play 42
Beautiful beast 43
Bel canto 44
Speranza 45
Thing with feathers 46
La dolce vita 47
Recital 48
Cockshut 50

Act III: Interludes
Criss-cross 53
Felt 54
Burial 55
Human Footprint Series: Snow 56
Human Footprint Series: Western Chorus Frog 57
Human Footprint Series: Horse Latitudes 58
Rehearsals: Mastery 59
Rehearsals: Sight-reading 60
Rehearsals: Reflection in five acts 62

Act IV: Summer
Table d'hôte 65
Ultima Thule 66
The day after 67
Down at the farm 68
Putting by 69
At Grandma's farm, after fighting with his brother,
    Onno lies in bed 70

Halifax　71
　　Popcorn　72
　　Off-leash　73
　　Radio days　74
　　Fog　75
　　Chez Toutou　76
　　Frère Jacques　77
　　Boys　78

Act V: Autumn
　　Rosh Hashannah　81
　　Garage sale　82
　　Fulling　83
　　In praise of uxoriousness　84
　　The long marriage　85

Notes　87
Acknowledgments　89
About the author　91

Man undertakes no enterprise in vain,
and Nature can no longer defend herself against him.
—*L'Orfeo*, Act III

Indeed, there are many things used in good singing style that are written in one way
but, to be more graceful, are effected in quite another…
—Giulio Caccini, Le nuove musiche, 1602

Prologue

HOCHELAGA

Donny found her weaving on the river island—Ari,
mythic maiden, heavy braid hanging down her back.
Behind the castle of her loom she crossed threads
in ancient code: cotton, silk, hemp, and wire.
Though Jewish law forbade the blend of
wool and flax, Ari wove these too. Unaware
the Romans banned a woman with a spindle
from appearing in the square lest she curse the harvest,
she left her shuttle's quiet slide, windows open to river
breeze, to buy her rice and nuts on St. Laurent.
Her solitude woke in him solicitude. Is this why he chose
to save her, to set her—a jewel—in his firmament?

Early music

That summer Ari lay on the swept wood floor,
                      Donny played the harpsichord.
River heat rose around the island, clinging to them,
            sticky with newborn love.

In tall frosted glasses, he served cantaloupe
                crushed with ice and lime, red beans and quinoa
on earthen plates. Dampness entered, settled
        like the children they didn't yet know.
On the swept wood floor she lay her braid undone—
              Bach's inventions catching in her hair.

Chernobyl wedding, 1986

They'd always believed the world would end
in a bright blast, then blankness—
not malignant pinpricks, invisible,
not toxins salting eccentric winds.

A bright blast, then blankness
would deliver them of adulthood,
not toxins salting eccentric winds,
not a seep, a spill, a pox on all gardens.

Delivered to adulthood's mansion,
hidden in ligatures of love
while seeps, spills, poxes amassed,
they tuned their ears to shuttle and string.

They hid in ligatures of love:
veiled, Ari circled seven times her groom,
tuning her ear to shuttle and string.
Together they smashed the wineglass underfoot.

Veiled, Ari circled seven times her groom,
wrapping him in a shell of blessings.
They smashed the wineglass underfoot
to remember the temple that burned and fell.

Though they dwelt in a shell of blessings,
still sorrow reached its damp fingers—
a reminder of temples burning, falling,
low chairs, torn sleeves, unwashed hair.

Sorrow still reached its damp fingers,
and an arsenal of poisons prepared to lick them.
The low chair, torn sleeve, unwashed hair
waited at the top of the stairs.

Arsenals of poison prepare to lick them,
malignant pinpricks invisible.
At the top of the stairs it waits:
the end of belief in the world.

Act I: Winter

Argonautica

Donny doesn't think he's made decisions—
life's a hungry lion tracking prey. Each hour has a texture
and a name, but not a place to stop. If only he could cast himself
beyond time's grip, forward, backward, he wouldn't care—
escape the wax museum of the now without a scratch,
without being missed. Where would he go? Some risky thrilling era?
But with indoor plumbing and martinis. Would he be a firefighter,
secret agent, pitcher, a hero riding rocky seas? Orpheus drowning Sirens,
shielding grateful sailors with his sunburst Stratocaster and his song.

Feast and Famine

Donny can remember when Ari ate it all: pad thai
and paella, pulled pork and posole, veal stuffed with apples
and pâté de foie gras. Now she rejects his meat and all the rest.
From their plush days of courtship, he recalls melon slices
rolled in slivers of prosciutto followed by couscous,
osso bucco, or cassoulet, menus he'd spend days devising.

When did it change, what broth must he feed her, what seed,
how temper his own gut's twisting as he waits?

He blanches pearl onions for palak paneer and roasts
a baby pig on a spit until its skin crackles.

When, when will she feast with him again?

Orchard and Forest

Warp and weft, the world is so divided: half is sleeping
while the other half's awake; half—at most—are capable
of love, and more than half dead at heart. Half are hedgehogs,
the other, foxes. Which is why Ari sticks to the material
wisdom, *two sets of threads at right angles, interlocking,*
why she moves around her studio at night to read and muse
on the divide between utilitarian craft and Art, millennia
of women's work in cloth and clay. The radiators sing on this
cool night, but she can almost taste the spring. She loves best
the knots of blue veronica before Donny cuts the grass,
the early morning lull before he starts his music and his noise,
his singing as he grinds coffee beans, filling the house with skunk.

THE CLAY WE ARE MADE OF

Who's a hedgehog, who's a fox? Donny must be a fox,
the way he pokes around where least he's wanted,
coveting the cheese *and* grapes that dangle from above,
    then wanting more.
                     Does this make Ari hedgehog,
curled around one big idea?
                            What's the big idea?
he asks her, when she's cleaned the fridge, pitched
his weeks-old yogurt and the starter for his sourdough, gone green.

Who do you think you are? he asks. She'd like to know that, too.
Pay attention is what yogis say. Let husbands tend themselves—
    it's trees and grass and frogs she wants to save.

Black leather couch

on which she'd lain all fall, Ari's mother, like a dry leaf.
                              Its slippery crease swallowed everything:

crochet hooks paper clips receipts a postcard
                    from Ari's sister Sophie, 1992, her mother's words.

Get the radio, she'd say, pointing to a glass of water.
                            The rings fell off her fingers.

While she napped, Ari knitted, something she'd begun
                            at college, to keep awake during class.

Mother owned closetfuls of yarn,
                    so Ari helped herself. Now Mother slept

under a shawl and fretted when awake.
                        Do you believe in ghosts?

Click, click went Ari's needles.
                    Mother'd always demanded

the empirical. I believe in souls, said Ari.
                    That's what I meant. I've never been so scared.

She cried whenever Ari's dad got up
                        to get a glass of milk her pills a blanket.

By October she was always cold.
                          What did I do wrong? Why are they angry?

No one's angry, Mother. But Ari's tongue
                            was just a plug of dirt.

She stroked her mother's naked hand.
                        I'll never knit a tea bag again.

THE BOOK OF LIFE

Though Ari won't believe in God, she knows that something somewhere
must be counting—calories and carbon use, every inner tube she's ever burst,
every acid-crusted battery—somewhere there's a ledger for the damage
of existence: each bottle top and what it cost the Earth,
the atmosphere, accruing to the rubbish mountain of her soul.

Joy is only sugar, an empty source of energy, and happiness a fiction;
it's misery and guilt that architect the real. And the body,
the body's just another spring of discipline; something counts each lick,
each sip, each chew, each mile she runs with weights on arms and legs
up and down the neighborhood so early that she wakes the dogs.

Human Footprint Series: Artist's Statement

These mixed media tapestries engage with how human activity
alters life on Earth—with the effects of our exploitation, our prerogative
of excess, our belief that technology will save us.
Fusing traditional handweaving of natural fibers with other media
and techniques—felting, beading, embroidery, paint, ink,
and lamination—this series reacts to unfolding environmental catastrophe.
Climate change results in melting polar ice and accelerated storms.
"Honeycomb" and "Western Chorus Frog" respond to the witches' brew
of agricultural chemicals and landscape pesticides; "Detritus"
and "Horse Latitudes" catalogue the consequences of a consumer
culture addicted to plastics and redundancy; "Zebra" is a visual reply
to the importation of invasive species. Incorporating practices
of women makers from over the centuries, these works also call
into question the man-made boundary between Art and craft.

Mouths of babes

Ari's dyeing yarn in tea when Stephan lopes into her studio—
headstrong first-born, jeans too short again. Can he have a dollar
for the dollar store. What will you buy? though she can guess.
Cap gun. He studies tea leaves swirling in the sink. The air stretches.

Don't you have enough? *They're all broke.* She tries to squash the knot
of righteousness crawling up her throat. Hasn't she told him
about plastic, about waste? The garbage patch sprawled the width
of continents? Half a billion tons. When we throw away
it just goes somewhere else. He looks up, shoots her
with his eyes: *So it's over anyway, and it's your fault.*
Her fingers probe her pocket for some change.

Domestic Dirge

Ari damns dawn-to-dusk digging machine in the street every day but Sunday, laundry day. Damn laundry in dark drifts under the boys' beds, damn beds that never get made. Curse nightstand stacks of books and cocktail party small talk. Curse soccer games where Onno sits out three quarters, studies clouds the fourth; curse 3:00 a.m. sweat and racing pulse, toilet trip, water glass, drug-sleep dawn; damn weeks rushed of sun and sweet white orchards, moments that should last and petty things amassed (ratty rugs, leaky pipe, missing knob, Christmas cards); curse homework and tooth-brushing, piles of small clothes to give away; and damn the Tooth Fairy, who will never visit Stephan's bed again.

Supermarket Blues

Pop-Tarts, Cocoa Crisps, Kraft Dinner, chicken nuggets
is what they feed the kids, or rather, what the kids will eat.

Pork chops in a pinch, but no mashed potatoes and nothing
touching on a plate. Stephan eats strawberries, Onno grapes.

They feed most often from the towers at the supermarket's centre,
the cardboard glossy food machine, brandishments of cereal, crackers,
chocolate-covered anything, product-placed so they can run

ahead and lob brightly baubled boxes into the basket Donny follows,
somnambulant, beside himself, as if thrust out of hell,
                                              alone in smothering light.

Water cycle

Evaporation

It's snowing lightly. Stephan feels it
like fingers in his hair as he waits for Dad
to drive him to his lesson. He knows
Donny will sit in the hall, pretend
to read, but eavesdrop on each note.

Condensation

Going home, they stop for preserved lemons.
More tubs of yogurt and white cheese
than Stephan could ever hope to name.
In the car: *What did you learn today?*
The water cycle.
Again?

Precipitation

It's hard to figure: how can they keep
learning the same thing? Each year
they add a little, Stephan supposes.
Today no one knew about infiltration.
It was a trick question, Stephan says.

Infiltration

Stephan does his homework at the counter.
Donny cooks, cutting chicken, onion, pickled lemon,
humming the concerto Stephan's learning.
I set your recital date for June.
Stephan breaks the pencil tip, gets up to sharpen.

Runoff

Maybe he'll do it, pack his rucksack,
leave his books behind. Or only take a few.
Hide out on the mountain, in a tree,
sneak back when no one's home,
steal bread and cheese, leave
not a crumb trailing out the door.

Superhero lullaby

Sleep demands a story, Donny on his side on Onno's narrow bed.
Once upon a time, he whispers, there was a demigod.

What's a demigod? Half god, half human. Orfeo sang and played
his lyre so that lions rested at his feet; to follow him, rivers

changed direction. Then came the wedding day...Eurydice bitten,
the journey to the underworld to fetch her. Orfeo's song, Charon's sleep.

The deal with Pluto: Orfeo wouldn't look back. But then,
right before the exit, his mistake...

Then what? Onno's eyelids, soft as flour, lashes black as ants.
Then she disappeared. Donny doesn't mention Maenad claws,

how they tossed Orfeo's head into the river. *But why did he look back?*
Should Donny tell him how dumb adults can be?

He strokes his son's bath-damp head. No one knows.
What do you think? Onno's breathing tightens into thought...

She was a ghost—he couldn't hear her steps. So he didn't know?
Onno shakes his head, shuts his eyes, lets go.

By with it

By mid-winter, her mother's chart reads *nulla per orem*.
Who never ended sentences with prepositions,
who recited from *Evangeline* by heart,
played anything you asked for by ear, whose father
crossed the Pyrenees by luck, the Atlantic by ship,
survived by bread and wit. By and by they'll place pebbles
on his stone after prayers at his daughter's burial.

But now she tosses in her young-winged sleep,
calls for mother, sister. Now still
but breathing, still gripping Ari's hand.

Dry hand, bitter year. Nothing
by mouth now—and nothing from
the daughter's, no oath Ari can swear to
or believe, nothing to abide by.

BACKHOE

Sunday before visiting hours, Dad's a pirate,
singing with the parrot on his shoulder—
Ob-La-Di, Ob-La-Da, flinging gobs onto the griddle.
Spatula in hand, standing on a backward chair,
Onno listens to the sizzle and watches bubbles rise,
black dots the signal to flip over.

Behind a bed of rails, she sleeps, wigless.
her head a shock of feathers.
Onno, glad he doesn't have to kiss her,
leaves the card he made beside the bed
and travels to the window, climbs onto the chair.
Eight floors below, across the street,
a backhoe's parked, stabilizing legs
set on concrete and dirty snow.
Onno blows onto the glass,
draws a happy face. Erases it
before anyone can see.

Hospital Solitaire

What is her plaint, where lay the blame,
what can Ari say but she was loved,
a love that's shrunk her lungs into a coil.
Does emotion tug on thought, or not:
is it the other way: *I think, therefore I feel?*
Her new description of the real. Always rangy,
she's a giant by a shrunken bed, her mother—
not her mother—just a face above a lace collar.
Ari plays the game of red on black on red,
all questions subsumed in what the cards reveal.
The doctor's paid his call, white-coated, but no tie,
to help them face the facts. Gave the order, shook their hands.
Her father's frame slumps into a chair. Each round,
she shuffles, starts again—no keeping score—
until her chin droops to her chest. Father and daughter rest
within the soundings from the hall—droning voices,
ticking heels. They wake when Sophie storms
the quiet room, flushed, hair undone, scarf dragging
behind, her face a stricken template of their loss:
afflicted, angry, out of breath and time.

Shiva

Always two—two sisters
wearing the same dress
measuring more against less.
In their father's house they soap
mirrors, clean the fridge of rigid
foods, scrape the oven floor, wash sheets
and towels in case a cousin comes
to stay, vacuum behind the piano,
tie together stacks of mouldy books
to cart out to the curb.
Two, two. Who misses her most.
Ari lays her head on a silk scarf,
sips its fragrant spice. Sophie pins
a brooch inside her sweater,
strokes its cold stone.
Will they divide each teacup
from its saucer, divorce
each pair of shoes? Who judges
who has more, who
more to lose.

In memoriam: Sonata 1014

Donny plays like he's fighting for his life, like he's flushing a fever, saving orphans, damming a flooding river. Forgive the jagged attack. Play with the fury of the bereaved. Like soldiers they'd tried to communicate over static smoke. The war has no solution for marriage. Start with warning shots. Kandahar is the backdrop of the unconscious, broken walls where children pick bullet casings for play, where slow suicides approach in dusty cars. Bach needs no translation. Counterpoint's the universal language, and harmony is hot. Play like you're James Joyce. Morning traffic clears its throat. Next door, the rabbi's prayer harmonized by pigeons. The metronome is medicine. Play like an icebreaker cracking a path through a stiffened river. Play like you're Mont Blanc's pyramid gleaming above shredded clouds. Maybe they are Aristophanes' comic couple, two bodies sewn back to back, impossible lovers: gorge and starve, open and cold, poor and wrong. He's distracted by desire the way birds follow *the river of the threaded needle* south to Trois-Rivières. He's always stepping on his partner's toes. He's a soldier, a gunner, a sapper panicked by his own exploding bowels. Play like you're fighting for your wife. Music needs no translation. Bach said it's just hitting the right keys at the right moment. Now you're swimming, breathing with the ligatures, recalling the cadence. You thank the lamb for the yarn you follow, the sweaters she's knit you. The violinist's ornaments are perfect. Thank her for her sprezzatura. Thank the piano for its strings and forgive yourself yourself. You are filled with desire for the silent dark, the prayers of pigeons cracking your dreams, her hair sweeping your neck. Swimming back along the river, the needles of every pine and fir reach for you. Swimming back along the river is like being orphaned and reborn, following a bright umbilical of white water. Play like you're the hidden river buried metres below the whirling waters. Play like you've opened the river's mouth.

FUGUE

They fell into bed   she facing the wall
    he reached for her hair   dark as damp feathers

They fell into bed   two empty boats
    an ache in the throat   he reached for her hair

The dark was a needle   dripping its juice
    she faced the wall   waiting for sleep

An ache in the throat   dripped a dark juice
    the ribs were a harrow   He touched her hair

her hand rose, his   fell like a boat
    in water a feather   in darkness a needle

Ribs a harrow   face an ache
    touch a needle   sob a wall

Act II: Spring

THIN WISHES

Ari would drink a hole in water, drink it all: sweet
water, still water, water from a jam jar; she would swim

between two waters and never give up, never decide,
never climb to either shore. She would eat bean sprouts and apples,

celery and carrots, anything she could bite raw and chew alone.
She avoids the pricking whiskers, slipping tongue,
his stirring, slicing hands. She would stay

in pure parks of imagination, the world before
butchery and squalor, before fleshpot and fantasy:
her hunger a single sinew stretched hard under skin.

MINATORY SPRING

Boy-blond Will—Ari's high school collision,
                                      an afternoon in May
that softened into evening. His white shirt and bleached jeans
                                      glowed like bones
against the park's thickening green. She noted
                                      the blue facets of his irises,
his palaver, finger dance, quick tongue licking the spliff's edge.
                                    They stopped to smoke
between the library and its conservatory, blooming
                                      from red Victorian brick
like a whalebone corset, hothouse plants pressed against the glass.
                                    Many times had Ari
walked that mulchy path, smelling what she smelled right now.
                                    That peat-steeped smell joining the tobacco
and the hash, joining other childhood smells: leather book jackets,
                                    yellowed vellum, ink and dust,
lilacs ripening in the yards. A piece of twine hooked below her navel,
                                    led her into the sad labyrinth of sex.

Sour teeth

Driving to the dentist Donny listens to the radio:
the Milky Way would taste like raspberries, which both delights
and saddens him. His interstellar pastures lie behind him—
he'll never savour the ambrosias of space. In the waiting room
a women's magazine affirms everything's recycled: recipes
for chocolate cake and how to drive your man wild. When did she
stop trying? Those mineral explosions of his lust return:
how he craved her taste—underarms, cunt, he licked
her freckles, folds, all the lonely fabric of her skin.

LECTURE ON THE ORIGINS OF MUSIC

Back in the day, no artiste, no narrow niche—
everyone could pluck a string, knock on wood
or skin, let the devil out, the angel in, obey
octaval law, shake the cosmic arcana's holy vibes.
Before tempered modulations, before sadness
sidled into minor keys, music was our thing.
Creation was nothing if not sonic: louder
than a thousand unstopped organs. The Earth sings
Mi Fa Mi (so *mi*sery and *fa*mine hold sway,
that joker Kepler wrote), the C-7th chord a match
for orbital ratios. Music *is* the sex of planets—
Shiva and Shakti fucking, their ghost notes
rattling the universe's springs.

The Male Gaze

Donny crosses campus looking for a treat.
April *is* the cruelest month, he thinks—
trees put forth, pansies widen velvet eyes.
His own eyes feel like weary slits between
parentheses. The cruelest cut is women, girls—
for what is he if not a boy—parading naked
arms and legs, breasts peeking out like balls of cream
from pastry shells, or small and loose.
Skirts, straps, sandals, shorts. All that glowing,
all that smooth. He weighs, which one?
Though *he'd* never—they'd always been the ones.

Café crème in hand, he turns to a contralto, *Professor Backus?*
Fifties sweater set and pearls, ironically deployed.
Pretty enough face, but flaccid. She bats her doll-glass eyes.
Something fun this summer? Oh, you know. The usual.
No need to tell her all his plans: research, auditions, rehearsals,
Nova Scotia. And you? He's stirring,
diverted by her summer charms: shorter skirt,
sweetheart neck, no bra. His brain hamster-scrambles—
Chamber ensemble? Chorus? Early Music History?
That's it: last year, her smartish paper on women singers
in the Gonzaga court. Monteverdi's *L'Arianna*, a warning
against women choosing husbands for themselves.
Marika! he almost shouts, and in reply she lilts,
Know anyone who needs a babysitter?

Montreal limestone

Dad's friend Bea leads them on a fossil tour of the Square Mile.
Onno fidgets, twists from Donny's hand, but Stephan's rapt:
they're standing in a coral sea. Spongy creatures spun
and circled salty waters. Larger creatures swallowed them.
Five hundred million years dissolved their splintered shells
to limestone five hundred metres thick. From this mottled grey
and pockmarked matrix bankers and industrialists built mansions.
Another kind of treasure's cached in Bishop Street's stone walls:
brachiopods, cephalopods, horn coral, sunflower, sea snail,
the city's silent chroniclers sank themselves in lime,
while moss animals scratched pale broken branches
into Scottish sandstone, ballast cast at port by ships
arrived to carry beaver pelts for European hats.
And what about that paw print in red brick, Onno points.
Bea hugs herself and laughs—just a cat chasing
through a brickyard, a mere century ago.

None the wiser

Stephan sails his bike down Esplanade,
first time this spring. Turns right at Rachel,
stalls to watch ten stocky men play soccer.
Crosses Parc first time himself—
greets the angel, face stained by winter pigeon shit.
Here, drummers throng in summer, hippies dance, Ari warns him
not to go alone. He *is* alone and riding. Dad raised the seat
and said *okay*. Delicious burning in his thighs, click
of tripping gears, past blowing bags and bits of trash
released from winter freeze, past sullen couples,
mongrel dogs, he pushes up the hill alone, lungs on fire,
crests the top and coasts the ramp toward the lookout's plaza.
He stops. He breathes. Below, the city: high-rises, chimneys, bridges,
steeples, narrowed streets where cars are toys. His face is dusty, throat is dry.
Turns to find a fountain. There, on the Chalet steps, Uncle Hugo
holding hands with someone, not Aunt Sophie.
Eyes meet, hands drop.
Hugo whispers in her ear, then smiles, calls Stephan's name.
So tall, he says. It's true, Hugo's shrunk, his favorite uncle,
who'd grabbed them up in blankets, galloping dizzy
round the flat, made them try Turkish delight, its feel and taste
of powdered roses forever bound with musty pipe and aftershave.
He introduces Mary, offers ice cream. They sit silent
in the wicked breeze. *What you doing this summer?*
Visit Granny, Nova Scotia. *Maurice goes to music camp. You too?*
Stephan shrugs. He and Maurice used to be best pals,
but lately everything has shifted. Boys he thought were friends
don't nod hello at school and rarely call.

He coasts his bike behind the house where Ari's raking beds.
Good ride? He nods. *You feel okay? Just thirsty. What's that?*
Stephan looks down: chocolate smear on his white T.

FOR EVERY LOCK A KEY

Ari's dream, which she doesn't understand, begins
like pricks of summer rain against a screen:

she's at a farm stand choosing vegetables, but everything
is steel and white—a meat market, men behind the counters.

She reaches for an artichoke but doesn't find a tight one,
flower firmly closed, teeth tucked in.

An aproned man behind the cold case points toward a pile of zucchini,
about to rot. *Free,* he tells her. No, she says. *How about a pint of peas?*

She takes them—freshly shelled—clutches the green basket to her chest,
yearning for a thistle's deeply lobed and arching silver leaves.

PERENNIAL

In bed with lilies of the valley, campanula,
bleeding hearts, breeze against her neck,
Ari smells the browning lilacs, feels a pressure coming on, a sneeze—
the description of orgasm she read long ago—a building
then release, like insight. Digs a hole for foxglove,
a poison leaf she's never dared to plant before.

Theories of play

From her garden Ari hears indoor discord: Stephan won't pick up his bow.
Not fair, then stomping on the stairs. He'll read in bed: comics, wars, submarines.
All talent, no drive. On a sun-streaked Saturday, he wants to ride his bike,
not press four strings into his cheek. Orpheus didn't have Xbox,
rollerblades, a soccer ball. In the sandbox, Onno commands
the red Frontloader, rolls it up and down the dunes. Donny's harpsichord
teases out the window. Will it tempt the boy downstairs to play?
Ari tucks parsley into soil, her own low aria garnishing the chords.

Beautiful beast

Up in the loft, Donny prizes the organ's grandiloquent
austerity, unbroken spokes of time he's most himself,
stripped down to fingers pressing manuals, feet
treading pedals, and he's back inside his father's church,
blooms of frost against the mullioned panes.
A calling, said his father. The whole orchestra of registers—
pipe-songs, delicate, robust, absurd—able to climb higher
than a mosquito's whine. Truth is, it tames him, returns him
to his sense that craft is core: the counting of the bars
in time, collapsing time, his breath, the wind—a birr.

Bel canto

Auditioning sopranos. Donny wants their voices
clear and lean. Whether cocky, meek, stout, or graceful,
he draws from each her gifts. The best know how to juggle breath
past the cords, to lift the palate like a cat and spin. He needs surprise
and colour: mahogany, apples, shadow, brass; he must have Callas,
Schwarzkopf, Sutherland. If their cheeks, their teeth, their eyes,
if all be flushed and glistening, if his hand might draw her water
from its well, paint sun-sliced clouds on chapel vaults—
as if they, he, anyone, still believed in angels.

Speranza

With her voice—cloudless sky, chocolate
lifted to lips, hummingbird hover,
twelve true notes and counting...up, up,
kite-pull, bellied sail, brass bell,
fourth and fifth drops
of rain on gables, spoon against
saucer, breath against ear, cool fingers,
hot broth, swig of bourbon, neat—

his day begins.

THING WITH FEATHERS

I.

Next morning, Donny floats
around the neighborhood tethered to the dog.
Lilac spice inflates his lungs, head light,
legs loose, can't believe, what luck.
Last night he found his Musica, his Eurydice!
He still feels her voice inside his chest,
a bee inside a flower bell.
Sally, always Sally,
never Sarah, so she said. Sally,
his saffron, his sandalwood, his salt.
Dark and quiet, much like Ari,
as she used to be. Teachable, trusting—
Gwenny tugs, stops to sniff, anoints the heads
of sunny daffodils. Then there was the boy,
waiting in the pews, his face the mirror of a god's.

II.

He auditioned, too. Boyfriend? Hard to tell.
He'd advertised for baritones, but thus far only tenors.
Losing hope until this scarecrow, doppelgänger
of the kid you'd want your daughter to bring home,
eager faced, corkscrew curled. Donny sounded
the intro to "Rosa del ciel," nodded for him to begin:
an oil-fall of clear Italian, generous range,
little rough in the dynamics—but that's work Donny loves.
He was tempted there and then to tell him yes, to offer him the bride.
Too young? To hear him better, Donny closed his eyes:
quick, light, and rich at once, soufflé *and* nightcap,
hot rum with butter and brown sugar. A soothing jolt.
Took up his pen, recorded number.
Let him suffer, let him wait.

La dolce vita

Getting dark when Donny almost stumbles on the sleeping
drunk who blocks the steps between two strips of grass.

Who slurs, *Hello Father*. But Donny's no brother,
no priest, just directs the music in this limestone pile,
Neo-Gothic with a dash of Arts and Crafts.
He enters, locks the door behind him,
switches on the transept lights, climbs to the loft,
the lungs of this cool cell. There's the Credo painted high.
Over the keys, he rubs his hands to warm them.

What is Donny's creed. Must he suck
a kiss from every cup before he goes?

Recital

Stephan sits beside Maurice in a chancel pew,
pulling at his cuffs. They wait their turn—
after babies playing piano or squeaky violins.
Why did Bach write so many pieces; not enough
to have two dozen kids? A little girl in blue
rises to play, but loses nerve, runs to her mum.
Could be a smaller him. He'd run if he could move.
Swallow if he could swallow. He sees Aunt Sophie
enter through the heavy door, her hair a nest, jacket
wet with rain. She finds a pew several rows behind
Hugo, who moves to sit beside her, but she blocks
the empty spot with her bag. Her gaze is fixed on stage,
where Stephan and Maurice must now ascend.
They tune strings, fall into the rhythms of their duo,
trade the theme as if a ball between them. Climax,
flourish, a pause before the silence. Applause.
Endorphin-flushed they smile, bow, head off stage.
Stephan thinks the practice almost worth it now.
He turns to congratulate Maurice, but he's grabbed
his cello, headed for the door, where his parents
seem to push him out, ahead of them, into the rain.

Cockshut

is what Donny's mother called this cradle between death
of day and birth of night. Donny climbs the shaky ladder
to his kitchen garden on the garage roof, waters chard and spinach,
surveys the city's electric skin and veins. Bursting from the trees,
cicada noise, zero to crescendo in four seconds.
In the neighbours' garden, the Hassidic father yells in Yiddish
at his teenage son. Donny's not sure whom to root for,
father now himself. Never mind his lack of comprehension,
it's the same: *Why didn't you?* in a Germanic strain.
Even if you haul those steep steps up
after you, no purchase, no roost is safe.

Act III: Interludes

Criss-cross

Castle and heddle the warp the weft
a web a cloth a nap the stuff
take yarn manila sendal and cross
tufts of rabbit merino floss
fiber worsted linen and jute
throw down a pattern unravel a suit
of sea water nacre opal and clay
plaited ribbons steeped in dark tea
skeins of skin brocaded bones
a bolt of tulle a pile of stones
milk and sugar a cotton web
a veil of clouds a coat of reeds
cut the length leave hang the thrum
fray the fringe abandon the loom

Felt

Freed from weft and heddle,
Ari layers strips of roving,
soaks them in soapy water,
pressing them into a mesh
she can lift off the table
and roll in bamboo matting,
squeezing and turning, binding
the strands 'til they're wound
tightly as watch springs,
spindles and fascicles
twisted in cellular coils.

Her breath is the music of kneading,
of hands pressing the fabric.
The stress of shoulders and fingers,
knuckles red in the water.
Is it a marriage this felting,
with all of the seams disappearing
where fiber fuses to fiber
forgetting the field it was raised in?

And is it wrong to desire
only this tolling inside her
until she's an empty well,
a pair of hands, wringing?

BURIAL

Ari's made a white thing—pale oblong of linen warp crossed
in wool and cotton, old lace bits from her grandmother's veil.

Onno finds her in the garden, digging. New greening leaves
smell like bugs and varnish. *What are you doing?*

Round her head, his mother wears a kerchief, knotted at the nape.
Even when her eyes are red, she's pretty. *I'm burying this cloth.*

Onno fetches his blue shovel. *Do you want help?*
The cloth glows on the short grass.

Why do you want to bury it? When Grandma was buried,
Stephan told him, an elevator lowered the coffin into a hole.

Each grown-up said something in Hebrew, threw shovelfuls of dirt.
Just for a little while. I want to distress it.

Why does his mother want the cloth to look sad?
Together they shovel until she asks him to stop.

She lays the cloth into the small grave. They cover it
with dirt and stones. *You can jump on it,* she says.

Soon he will be six. From under the porch, he fetches his rope,
arcs it overhead, skips into its blurred orbit.

Human Footprint Series: Snow

Let the zone of perpetual snow not disappear. Let the world be white: from Chibougamau to Blanc-Sablon, from Drummondville to Lac-Saint-Jean, from Matagami to Rivière-du-Loup, let candles of snow light forests and flakes descend in capes and saucers, sleepily silver and white. Remember how it began: from school windows in naptime hush we watched as chalk dust shook loose from plump skies, then cupfuls of rice, rabbit fur, knucklebones, chipped china, and finally a haze of hectic feathers. By the time we got off the bus, it had grown into a hungry animal, clung to dormer and sill, banked against thresholds, piled high on driveways where we drilled into drifts with shovels, mittens crystal-pilled with hard beads of sweat. The city sank into its calm. Breathing smoky cauls, we stood still in the descent of the last slow roses. What did we know of tepid rains to come: no meringue, no global à la mode, no frozen zenith or satin skullcap with which to honor the divine. You'll recall toes curling in wet socks and the ore-filled windows of houses leaning into dark. Blown bits pricked your skin. Stepping into the plain wooden room, the heave of heat, you shut the cold behind you. How you laid stiff mittens on the radiator's hiss, looked up to see your family, each settled by the fire with a book, faces caught in concentration, each reading a different story.

Ari Backus 2006
Hemp, wool, thumbtacks,
goose down, tinsel, mirror,
charcoal, frozen nettles
120 x 190 centimetres

Human Footprint Series: Western Chorus Frog

Upon mansions usurping marshland, upon springs ever warmer
by degrees and sooner, let curses fall, and let frog no longer breed
by river's edge, nor leave egg sac under sodden forest logs, neither
in lake's reedy shallows. Let frog not sing nor her children sing springtime
comb and fingernail, nor chew mosquito on humid nights. Not even protect
your bedchamber, your kneading board. Over frog-corpse roadways,
his petal underbelly absorbing poison from runoff ditch and golf course,
let sorrowful sound rise. Let male be made female by chemical castration,
and as her song evanesces, let your cradles empty, empty, empty.

> Ari Backus, 2006
> Felted wool, grass, reeds, acrylic,
> foil, lightning bugs, birth control
> pills, beads, rain, moss
> 100x80 centimetres

Human Footprint Series: Horse Latitudes

Thus does it enter the food chain: picnic straw,
party favor, six-pack collar, a baubled slaw
forms the Great Pacific Garbage Patch—elastic gyre,
litter-midden, invisible to satellite photography
despite its size and density, a mass of hidden particles,
broken down by water's flux and flow to toxic sludge
and *mermaid's tears*, fine plastic pellets resembling
fish eggs. This soup's consumed by filter feeders—
barnacle, worm, squirt, and flea—who nourish
sea turtles, seals, and those mythical birds
whose dance is a chorus of castanets, beak on beak,
of hoots and calls, and quick neck-tuck to fluff
an underwing. They mate innocent of syringe,
of toothbrush, chosen from this pile of dross
to choke their feeding chicks—
these Cleopatra-eyed Laysan albatross.

                            Ari Backus, 2006
                            Paint, rags, string, grocery bags,
                            screen-door mesh, twist-ties, bottle
                            tops, shells, feathers, condoms, fish
                            bones, ambergris
                            100x120 centimetres

Rehearsals: Mastery

Donny envies her the order of her threads, neatness of the loom, palettes of skeins piled high. Compare this to the score he must unwind, ingest to play by heart. The orchestra accompanying the voices *is* Orfeo's lyre. So many birds to catch: what is *his* vision and how transmit it. Atmosphere or affect buoys the voices: flutes for shepherds, regal for ferryman. Or context: festive dances best on the guitar? He vacillates: a stage and costumes; or a modest room, a chamber piece? And which ending: the *lieto fine* of deus ex machina, Apollo saves his son; or the tragic classic, Orfeo massacred? Each possibility commends itself—as he wakes, while washing greasy after-supper pans, in grey minutes before sleep. It feels like adolescent agony, riding shotgun with his father, *A man wouldn't do a thing if he waited to be ready.*

Rehearsals: Sight-reading

Donny takes his singers through the score,
some old, some new. Always tensions
in the crew—competition for the solos.
For now he needs to blend their timbres,
arrange the best bouquet. His joke
about castrati fails, but he plugs on—
bangs out three times the toccata,
heavy-footing on the piano: *Imagine
sackbuts, lutes, cornetti, violins.*

Now legato, as La Musica invites
the audience. Lilting ritornelli
punctuate her song. Come happy shepherds,
happy nymphs—monody, duets,
and trios—accents shift, motifs repeat,
rhythms surge and evanesce.

Suddenly the plaintive messenger—*Your wife is dead.*

The chorus—*Mortals must not put their faith in joy.*

Listen how each scene is colored, he instructs—
Thracian fields, mixed voices
           above a bed of strings;
the regal's brassy reeds
           and the all-male chorus, Hell.

By the time they reach the chorus of infernal spirits
their sound begins to coalesce—
the ostinato of "Possente Spirto" echoes
Orfeo's arioso, while spectral Eurydice hovers.
Then the crash of thunder,
her wretched exit song.

At break they gossip, speculate
about that couple—why he turns.
An alto says, *He's pleading, feels unworthy.*
A counter-tenor mocks—
He didn't trust her.

Hall rented, orchestra engaged,
Donny sips his tea and listens
vaguely, making lists.

Rehearsals: Reflection in Five Acts

Although Orfeo loved only Eurydice,
at first she sent him packing
as if he were not a demigod who sang
like a thrush in rain after weeks of drought.
Easy to imagine the fields of Thrace,
a future forever filled with flowers—
jonquils and poppies blooming together—
and that love would vanquish all reason.

What note did Orfeo sound in Charon,
and who could predict such an ending?
The audience longed for their escape
(after the wedding under dripping wisteria).
Breathless, they reached Hell's portal—
Abandon all hope ye who enter here.

Abandon all hope ye who enter here.
Breathless, they reached Hell's portal.
After the wedding under dripping wisteria,
the audience longed for their escape.
Who would predict such an ending,
and what note did Orfeo sound in Charon?

Would love vanquish all reason?
Jonquils and poppies bloomed together,
a future forever filled with flowers.
Easy to picture the fields of Thrace.
A thrush in rain after weeks of drought—
he sang like the demigod he was.
At first she sent him packing, Orfeo,
though he loved—loved!—none but Eurydice.

Act IV: Summer

Table d'hôte

Before he takes the kids down east, Donny makes a meal:
the troupe is coming over, including Sally and her boy.
Donny's hardly given him a thought, but now—stirring
pine nuts over fire, checking pita, cracking breastbone,
laying the chicken flat—he does. Yesterday he made the garlic
sauce, mashed the eggplant, started homemade yogurt.
For dessert, small pastries stuffed with marzipan,
fried in oil, soaked three nights in orange syrup.
Tabouleh with fresh mint chills next to the prosecco.
He sees himself pouring, waiting for the fizz to calm.

Ultima Thule

Onno waits in bed for his story. Donny begins:

They think Phytheas travelled north to the farthest point of Scotland
or Iceland, or even Norway—a place where sea, mist, and land
became as one watery lung. *Couldn't see a hand before your face,
your grandpa would have said.* How Phytheas got to England,
they can only guess: probably through the Pillars of Hercules.
And what is that? asks Donny. The Strait of Gibraltar.
Onno feels his father smile in the dark. Then up the coast, across
the channel and along the southern shore to Cornwall
where he maybe traded goods for tin. Tell me how they made
the boat, Onno demands, even though he knows. It's called a curragh,
made of wickerwork—a giant basket bound in buttered oxhides
and waterproofed with pitch. How did he navigate? Sun and the North Star,
and a gnomon, a wooden staff. Measured shadows from it with a string.
Maybe next week at Grandma's they'll build one on the beach,
get lost in the bay's mix of water, land, and fog—one watery lung, lung, lung—

but first Onno floats into his lonesome sleep. Ribs, branches on a tide.

The Day After

Ari's scrubbing at the sink
the tablecloth from last night's meal.
From behind, he lays a hand on her shoulder,
I told you I'd take care of it.

Why this one? (Shit—wedding present,
hand-embroidered, from some Moroccan aunt,
royal blue on white, for summer meals.)

She's just a girl! (Now it dawns
on him—Sally.) *She's just a voice,
Nothing more. If I can help—*

She looks directly in his eyes:
*Remember what I said
about babysitters?
Same thing for sopranos.*

Donny turns away from sink,
red stain against the blue and white.
Nothing he can say that wouldn't open ruin's door.

Down at the Farm

In this house great-grandfather built,
replacing what he'd called a carpenter's catastrophe,
live Donny's mother and her sister in grey girlhood.
A clean life in the valley, growing cukes and corn and berries,
putting pickles up and jams, staffing their own farm stand
through October. Donny takes a volume off the shelf,
The Story Book of Food, 1933. Blue mottled cover,
spine worn to linen at the ends. He opens it: while rabbit
looks calmly on, Stone Age Boy builds a fire, an Egyptian
snares a bird, and farmers learn to plow. A cock crows,
a tractor starts, it all begins again somehow.

Putting By

Stephan won't share a bed with Onno, so Donny does,
wakes to find the child curled catlike at his feet.
Donny rises, pees, lifts blinds onto the valley's
foggy calm, smells his mother's baking. His childhood's
a step into that kitchen where they fed him cinnamon twists
and berry buckle, taught him to pare apples, cut in lard,
gave him fairy tea. Today he'll take the boys out picking,
put up pies to freeze. Why should he? They have enough.
Just to hear it in her voice, mid-winter
when she calls—*We had a treat tonight.*
Just to hear this summer's juice on her tongue.

At Grandma's farm, after fighting with his brother, Onno lies in bed

Before thunder, trees wrestle with the rain.

Onno longs for swaddling, something fast
to hold him down, to stop him rolling
like an empty bottle in a speeding car.

When the fat cat jumps onto his chest,
(outside, dark leaves still dripping),
he's sure it's heard a signal from his mind.

Halifax

Beatrice, who can read him, who knows Donny left the boys back at the farm,

who can see it all, after the rehearsal, the last before the concert, the troupe at a waterfront café,

who smiles as he sips a local beer, repeats *the opera's a mirror*, gestures like an actor to the sea, the setting sun,

who, because they slept together once (while conservatory classmates, before their marriages, before her stillbirths), doesn't miss

when Sally's laugh catches at him like a burr on wool, who doesn't say aloud, *two besotted shepherds (or no, three)*,

doesn't ask how Ari's doing because she knows (still sad, still missing),

upon whom nothing's lost, not how the girl laughs so hard at one boy's joke, she spills wine on the other's sleeve, nor how he doesn't seem to mind.

Whose silent eyes say, *Donny, don't let it go to water,* who's guessed the unseen in the seen, who understands, *she's made herself a bed inside his ear.*

Popcorn

Anticipation's cross-stitch wakes her
like the histamine injection of a bee,
like a hangnail Ari knows she shouldn't pull.
Pleasure's better with delay, that knot, the secret
salty canker the tongue can't help but reach for.
Yet in the empty house, she skips her stretch,
her walk, her tea, moves straight to cut
from loom her latest piece. Audience
and director both—the velvet curtain rising.

OFF-LEASH

Watching Gwen-the-Corgie check out the dog run,
Ari meets a man she hasn't seen before.
It's 3:00 p.m. Shabby beard, unwashed hair,
pajama bottoms, leather jacket, a cigarette—
disgusting habit—punched between his lips.
But the dog's a sweet low mutt, mix of lab
and shepherd he calls *Toutou* in a tender voice
and plays with like a puppy. Ari rocks from side to side
while they watch the dogs sniff end to end,
exchanging facts. Jean, his name is, lives
two blocks away, and when he exhales
his mouldy breath and smiles she thinks
this just might be the perfect time to smoke.

Radio days

Sometimes a door slides open.
Ari's listening to Berg's chromatic scale—
Lulu—and she's back to 1980, the Met,
standing room behind the orchestra, Donny's
cotton sleeve against her arm.

Stratas's voice was a tunnel—
once entered, she never wished to leave.
At intermission, when the minks
went home—no dissonance in
suburbia—Donny led her
to the second row, where she heard
the opera's mirror reverse itself.
Into depravity sank Lulu:
queen of danger, doll of darkness,
apple of all eyes, she sang until
Jack arrived to rip her song
in two. They rode the subway back
to the Bowery, ate verenyky,
kissed each other madly on their friend's futon,
slept replete in the city's simmering hum.

Fog

Sleep is a country to which he can't obtain a visa.
In darkness Donny reaches for his robe, wanders
to the kitchen where he warms a cup of milk, something his mother
did that he used to think was foolish. He pours it in the smallest
of her three tin pots, white enamel splashed with orange flowers,
handles glossy black. He's always loved these three,
the way they nest reminds him of the milk and eggs and cheese
they used to make here at the farm, back when he fed corn
to leghorns, learned to press a wood-cut cow into butter bricks.
Sweet steam fogs his glasses as he raises a mug to old wives.

Chez Toutou

Jean's ground floor Plateau railroad flat—
double parlours off the hall, Buddhist altar,
red Che poster. Ari washes hands:
scum on backsplash, thinning towel.
The small yard with crates for chairs,
zucchini and tomatoes, a lawn of mint—
crushed fresh for tea, honey from his bees.
He fetches the smoker, netted hats, slides
a centre frame out, *doucement, doucement,*
revealing the central disk, eggs, larvae,
sealed brood cells, the upper corners crammed
with pollen, honey. *Ne bouge pas,*
he says, and with the lightest touch
moves from her hand a bee
she hadn't felt.

Frère Jacques

The house is dark and hot and quiet
Ari opens windows showers
looks into the mirror her dripping face
her long thick hair takes up
her finest shears begins to cut
small chunks enjoying the slicing sounds
until she is Falconetti's silent Joan
and lighter-headed finds her cooler bed
now easier to sleep in
                    Church bells wake her
Over dawn's glancing clouds
they strike the dip between
her clavicles knocking night over
to hollow out the morning stitching
up the absence between hours
like starlings pitching shadows
over English moors a black body
pulling flocks into its net
one bell waking another the city
carolling its songs

BOYS

When through the open door
they come she's at the stove
stirring harira, the soup
her mother made after the fast—
Mum, you look like a boy.
She bends to Onno's touch.
After plates are washed and stacked,
kids asleep, she lets Donny touch it too.

Act V: Autumn

Rosh Hashannah

Autumn trees thrill unspeakable
stretching their branches, shameless.
Pretending wood is unbreakable,
the autumn trees thrill unspeakable:
lit from hot coals, Sugar Maple,
belle of the north, soon undresses—
autumn trees thrill unspeakable,
stretching their branches. Shameless.

Garage sale

Ari's father, who collected seeds and stories, taught her
frogs, birds, trees, flowers, dumps the frozen soup into a pot,
her mother's pot, her mother's soup, *the last she made*, he sighs.
Ari lifts a piece of bread, but doesn't bite.

It's out to shelves of grimy vases, hoarded jars
and sodas bought on sale, typewriter, a broken mower
blade next to the freezer chest (that crypt).
On hooks several work hats, dust-stiffened and dry
as hide, her father's leather field coat.
Continents of oil map the concrete slab poured
on Ari's seventh birthday. Fresh, it formed
a rectangle divided into four; even now she thinks
chocolate bar. Before it cured, her father
took her hand, coated it in salad oil, pressed it
in a corner by the door. He passed an awl
to scrawl her name with in an arc.
See, there it is, under last fall's rusted leaves.

FULLING

Time tips its pitcher spins
its reel red and yellow
leaves wheel to land
reveal green veins Ari washes
one last time the weavings
for her show pins them to
the line new cold biting her
breath leaves them flapping
knots and seams exposed
like those other naked ladies
spreading in their loamy bed
at the foot of the back porch stairs
purple petals cool skins

In Praise of Uxoriousness

Let husbands be lush with lovingkindness, doting tongues, private smiles, satisfied withal. Let them bless and polish with deft thumbs the prehistoric, heart-bottomed goddess unburied from volcanic ash. Offer back rubs, grapes, and satin slippers; swell her caves and curves to give and receive pleasure without shame. Let them follow like a drone its queen, a string its kite, a wave its shore, a dog the scent of every grass blade and fence post. Invite her to lie together on a leafy couch, crush lavender between her breasts. Admire her eyes (like gazelles) and teeth (like goats). Be not the fox that spoils the vineyard, nor the gardener who won't treasure his own lilies. Breathe her hills of myrrh, bathe her feet in milk, eat of the honeycomb, reap that most intimate, spectacular fruit.

THE LONG MARRIAGE

Lilac-crowned Amazon, birthday gift from thirty years ago.
Ari doubts her mother knew how long a parrot lasts, or how
his chromosomal structure would make him flirt with men, not her,
who only gets his jealous peckings. Still, it's hard to keep herself
from stroking his iridescent mauve, his ruby splashes.

Donny built a roost from bolted plumber's pipe, wooden dowels,
and old refrigerator shelves where perches Prince, calling for his breakfast:
chopped almonds, carrot sticks, and apples. Open, Stone Beak.
Extend, Black-Bean Tongue. Master settles to his own bowl—
yogurt and granola—and listens to the music of his best-fed child.

Notes

The epigraph from *L'Orfeo* is an amalgam of translations by Avril Bardoni and Alessandro Striggio.

"Hochelaga" is thought to be the name of the indigenous village Jacques Cartier encountered when he arrived in the vicinity of what is now Montreal.

"In memoriam: Sonata 1014" is inspired by Bruce Smith's supersonic collection, *Devotions*, in particular "Devotion: Red Roof Inn." The phrase "the river of the threaded needle" is taken from the Wikipedia article on the Saint-Maurice River.

"By with it": The title comes from an old expression noted in the *Oxford English Dictionary*'s definition of *by*: "Of a person: done for, ruined, dead: esp. in to be by with it."

"Lecture on the origin of music" takes much of its language and information from the last chapter of David Byrne's *How Music Works*.

"Montreal limestone" takes inspiration and some language from Ingrid Birker's article, "What Buildings Tell: Fossils Hidden in Plain View," published in the Fall/Winter 2013 issue of *Ornamentum*.

"Human Footprint Series: Horse Latitudes": Much of the material in this poem comes from a Wikipedia article on the subject of the Great Pacific Garbage Patch.

"Halifax": The quotation at the end of this piece is a modified translation of *und machte sich ein Bett in meinem Ohr* (Rilke, *Sonnets to Orpheus: I, 2*, trans. Stephen Mitchell).

"Fog": The first line of this poem is a modified line from Ann Patchett's novel, *Bel Canto*.

Poems about Monteverdi's opera *L'Orfeo* owe a good deal to the research of scholars whose essays appears in *Claudio Monteverdi: Orfeo,* edited by John Whenham. Thanks as well to Ole Meyer for his companionable correspondence on the opera and to my colleagues Heather Buchman, Lydia Hamessley, Rob Kolb, and Sam Pellman, for their musical tutelage. Other insights came from liner notes of audio and DVD recordings. Any mistakes or misinterpretations, accidental or purposeful, are entirely my own.

Ari's "Human Footprint Series" takes its name from "The Human Footprint," a multi-media series of tapestries by fiber artist Deborah Weir, and I thank her for her generous help and inspiration.

Acknowledgments

Many thanks to the editors of the following publications in which versions of these poems appeared, sometimes in different forms and under different titles: *Arc* ("Early music," "*Argonautica,*" "The book of life," "Black leather couch," "Human Footprint Series: Western Chorus Frog," "Backhoe," "The long marriage," and "Cockshut"), *Chirograph*, the *Toronto Review of Books* blog ("Sour teeth"), *The Cincinnati Review* ("Thin wishes" and "Domestic dirge"), *Gastronomica* ("Feast and famine," "Supermarket blues," "Table d'hôte," and "Putting by"), *The Literary Review of Canada* ("Human Footprint Series: Snow" and "In memoriam: Sonata 1014"), and *The Malahat Review* ("Theories of play," "Beautiful beast," and "Bel canto").

"Human Footprint Series: Horse Latitudes" was displayed in the travelling textile exhibit, "Confluence," curated by Deborah Weir and Inga Buell. Thanks to Jody Gladding for the suggestion of adding a materials list to each of the Human Footprint poems.

I'm indebted to the many generous readers who have helped bring Donny and Ari to life: Pat Corbus, Cindy Day, Patrick Donnelly, Jamie Gaetz, Marianne Janack, Betsy Kepes, Ann Scott Knight, Gary Leising, Eileen Moeller, Alex Pierce, Andrew Rippeon, Jane Springer, Margie Thickstun, James Wells, Vicki Schmolka, Mary-Sherman Willis, and Jamie Zeppa.

Many thanks to my editor Sue Chenette for her spirit of diligent and patient collaboration, to Alayna Munce for her excellent copy-editing, to the production crew at Brick Books, and to Kitty Lewis, general manager extraordinaire.

My thanks goes as well to several institutions for their support: The Canada Council for the Arts, the Ledig-Rowohlt Foundation for my stay at Château de Lavigny, the Vermont Studio Center, and Hamilton College.

And as always, unending gratitude to my family, who support and inspire my work in so many ways, especially Jonathan, who lets me make a bed inside his ear. *Mil beijos.*

NAOMI GUTTMAN's first book of poems, *Reasons for Winter* (Brick Books), won the A.M. Klein Prize for Poetry. *Wet Apples, White Blood,* (McGill-Queen's University Press), was co-winner of the Adirondack Center for Writing's Best Book of Poetry for 2007. She has received grants from the Canada Council for the Arts and the Constance Saltonstall Foundation for the Arts, as well as an Artist's Fellowship from the New York Foundation for the Arts. She teaches English and creative writing at Hamilton College in Clinton, New York.